MI

THI

Torr
Equa
unus
back
See

Cast
The
med
to it
Piaz

Duo
It's t
the
of st
See

Tori
The
skyli
See

Tori
This
Miai
balc
Vial

Tori
Luig
qua
the
held
Piaz

Pirelli Tower
Ponti's 'Pirellone' is a beloved symbol of the
postwar boom years when modern design
took bold strides forward. He went big, too.
See p013

INTRODUCTION
THE CHANGING FACE OF THE URBAN SCENE

Depending on your perspective, Milan is either located in the south of northern Europe, or in the north of the south, which is why the locals, with their proximity to Switzerland, Austria and France, feel closer to the continent than the peninsula. Due to its reputation for fast-paced industry, work and progress, it is often claimed that the city is not as animated by food, family or free time as the rest of Italy (whether this is true is contentious), but it does align itself with the business hubs of Europe. Certainly, the flurry of development since Expo 2015, from a restaurant boom to clusters of bold skyscrapers, has imbued it with a more refined air. But this is a sophistication that belongs uniquely to this crossroads of culture.

Unlike Rome, Venice or Florence, Milan doesn't offer up its finest wares on a plate, so you'll have to work harder to uncover its gems. Many visitors come for the calendar events, including Fashion Week and the highly influential furniture show Salone del Mobile in April when any available space is turned into a showroom and the city is transformed. Others are drawn by the retail – there's nowhere better to shop, as the most enticing boutiques are close together and carry limited-edition lines that are rarely on sale elsewhere. The original beacon of luxury is the 150-year-old <u>Galleria Vittorio Emanuele II</u> (see p080), its frescoes and decor now fully restored – in Milan, a proper entrance and a *bella figura* are paramount. This is, after all, a place fixated by style, where looking your best is a way of life.

ESSENTIAL INFO
FACTS, FIGURES AND USEFUL ADDRESSES

TOURIST OFFICE
Piazza Castello 1
T 02 8845 5555
www.turismo.milano.it

TRANSPORT
Airport transfer to city centre
Urban Line 73 departs Linate Airport
every 10 minutes from 5.30am to 12.59am
(€1.50). Malpensa Express departs to
Cadorna or Central Station every 30
minutes from 5.25am to 1.30am (€13)
Car hire
Avis
T 02 8901 0645
Metro
www.atm-mi.it
Trains run from 6am to 12.30am (a 24-
hour pass is €4.50; 48 hours is €8.25)
Taxis
Radio Taxi
T 02 8585
Hailing a cab on the street is difficult, so
find a rank or call for a taxi

EMERGENCY SERVICES
Emergencies
T 112
Late-night pharmacy (until 9pm)
Farmacia Stazione Centrale
Piazza Duca d'Aosta
T 02 669 0735

CONSULATES
British Consulate-General
Via San Paolo 7
T 02 723 001
www.gov.uk/government/world/italy
US Consulate-General
Via Principe Amedeo 2-10
T 02 290 351
it.usembassy.gov

POSTAL SERVICES
Post office
Via Cordusio 4
T 02 7248 2508
Shipping
Mail Boxes Etc
Via Maddalena 1
T 02 6762 5544

BOOKS
Gio Ponti by Ugo La Pietra
(Rizzoli International Publications)
The Pursuit of Italy by David Gilmour
(Penguin)
A Traveller in Italy by HV Morton
(Da Capo Press)

WEBSITES
Art/Design
www.thatscontemporary.com
Newspaper
www.corriere.it

EVENTS
Cortili Aperti
www.adsi.it
Miart
www.miart.it
Salone Internazionale del Mobile
www.salonemilano.it

COST OF LIVING
Taxi from Linate Airport to city centre
€20
Cappuccino
€1.60
Packet of cigarettes
€5
Daily newspaper
€1.50
Bottle of champagne
€30

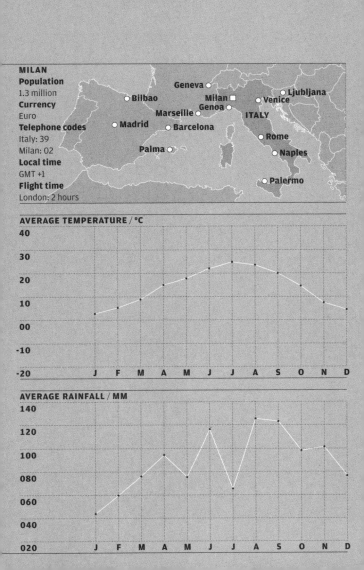

MILAN
Population
1.3 million
Currency
Euro
Telephone codes
Italy: 39
Milan: 02
Local time
GMT +1
Flight time
London: 2 hours

Geneva Ljubljana
Bilbao Milan Venice
Marseille Genoa **ITALY**
Madrid Barcelona
Palma Rome
Naples
Palermo

AVERAGE TEMPERATURE / °C

	J	F	M	A	M	J	J	A	S	O	N	D
40
30
20
10
00
-10
-20

AVERAGE RAINFALL / MM

140
120
100
080
060
040
020
J F M A M J J A S O N D

NEIGHBOURHOODS
THE AREAS YOU NEED TO KNOW AND WHY

To help you navigate the city, we've chosen the most interesting districts (see below and the map inside the back cover) and colour-coded our featured venues, according to their location; those venues that are outside these areas are not coloured.

MAGENTA
Come here to see Leonardo da Vinci's *The Last Supper*, which hangs in the beautiful convent of Santa Maria delle Grazie, the Museo Archeologico (Corso Magenta 15, T 02 8844 5208) and unorthodox design gallery Spazio Rossana Orlandi (see p070), for talent that is very much alive.

SEMPIONE
Castello Sforzesco (Piazza Castello) is filled with museums and beyond its moat, Parco Sempione is dotted with architectural gems including the Triennale (see p026), and the 1838 Arco della Pace, designed by Luigi Cagnola to celebrate Napoleon's victories. Corso Sempione is lined with chintzy bars.

PORTA ROMANA
Past the 16th-century arch is a laidback yet lively district. Highlights are the QC Terme spa (Piazzale Medaglie D'Oro 2, T 02 5519 9367), below the old city walls, Pasta Madre (Via Corio 8, T 02 5519 0020) and eaterie Un Posto a Milano (Via Cuccagna 2, T 02 545 7785) in the Cascina Cuccagna farmhouse.

CENTRO
The Duomo (see p014) sits at the heart of the metropolis, flanked by the magnificent Galleria Vittorio Emanuele II. Across the piazza is Palazzo Reale, the medieval seat of government, now host to significant art exhibits, and adjacent is the Museo del Novecento (see p077), with masterpieces by Umberto Boccioni and Carla Accardi.

PORTA VENEZIA
This is Milan's most eclectic neighbourhood, in which gay bars, and Indian, Korean and Ethiopian joints make for a spirited mix. In the glorious 1796 Villa Reale, the Galleria d'Arte Moderna (Via Palestro 16, T 02 8844 6359) shows 19th-century works and hosts the charming LùBar café (T 02 8352 7769).

BRERA/MONTENAPOLEONE
A former artists' quarter, now-smart Brera has design galleries, upscale shops and a flourishing food scene. In Montenapoleone, the Quadrilatero della Moda is a nucleus of luxury boutiques. You will also find the jewel-box historic house museum Bagatti Valsecchi (Via Gesù 5, T 02 7600 6132).

NAVIGLI/ZONA TORTONA
The city's remaining canals form the axes of nightlife in charming Navigli, where venues like Momento (Via Filippo Argelati 12, T 320 392 4528) and Rebelot (Ripa di Porta Ticinese 55, T 02 8419 4720) offer sophisticated concepts. The warehouses in Tortona have been colonised by creatives.

PORTA NUOVA/ISOLA
Ambitious urban planning and a coterie of starchitects have turned Porta Nuova into a towering business district. By contrast, low-rise, residential Isola has a bohemian energy that has inspired innovative, hip locales like Wood*ing Bar (Via Garigliano 8, T 391 474 4329) and Surlì (Via Genova Thaon di Revel 12, T 02 2222 2367).

LANDMARKS
THE SHAPE OF THE CITY SKYLINE

The historic core winds around the Duomo (see p014), with arteries radiating out to the ring roads. To the north is the monumental 1931 Stazione Centrale (Piazza Duca d'Aosta 1) and the revamped Porta Nuova district, lending diversity to the topography once dominated by Gio Ponti's iconic statement for Pirelli (see p013). Here, Torre Unicredit (Piazza Gae Aulenti) spirals to the city's highest point, near the 161m Palazzo Lombardia (Piazza Città di Lombardia 1) and KPF's soaring Torre Diamante (Via Mike Bongiorno), all linked by a landscaped promenade to Bosco Verticale (overleaf).

After the effort expended for Expo 2015, the city is now genuinely cosmopolitan. The original Fiera district, to the west, is home to the clunkily named CityLife, which completes in 2019, bookmarked by a trio of towers designed by Arata Isozaki, Daniel Libeskind and Zaha Hadid, known as The Straight One, The Curved One and The Twisted One respectively. To the south, the ancient 'Little Port' (for Milan's canals) of Darsena has undergone a makeover, and hosts a gourmet market and bars, with a landscaped waterside promenade between Navigli and Tortona. Then the industrial and repurposed warehouses give way to fields of rice and corn, and Lombardy's 18th-century farmhouses, some restructured as restaurants and cultural venues. Yet on a smog-free day, despite all this urban development and the fast-rising skyline, it is still the Alps that dominate.

For full addresses, see Resources.

Bosco Verticale

Another eye-catching Porta Nuova project, Bosco Verticale is a couple of residential towers 110m and 76m in height, rendered unorthodox by virtue of the 15,000 plants, 4,500 shrubs and 800 trees that soften the facade. Designed by Boeri Studio and built on a vacant lot, the high-rises propose a prototype for an environmental solution to Milan's density and air-pollution issues. This 'Vertical Forest' topped out in 2014 and its covering of greenery represents the equivalent of an entire hectare of foliage. The complexities of cultivating large trees on balconies rising up to 19 and 27 storeys necessitated a raft of engineering feats, as well as the implementation of a recycled grey-water irrigation system. Integrated photovoltaic panels provide energy.
Via Gaetano de Castillia/Via Federico Confalonieri

Torre Velasca

Much debated at home and abroad at the time of its construction, the 1958 Torre Velasca was designed by BBPR (Gian Luigi Banfi, Lodovico Barbiano di Belgiojoso, Enrico Peressutti and Ernesto Nathan Rogers). A remarkable take on a medieval fortress, it swells at the residential upper storeys to resemble a watchtower, and its cantilevered supports are an inverted nod to the Duomo's famous buttresses (see p014). The spacing of the windows is irregular, creating an interesting dynamic to the facade. The lobby is the only part of the building open to the public; after a stroll in the surrounding plaza, visit the nearby Rotonda della Besana (Via Besana 12), a deconsecrated late baroque church with an unusual curving colonnade, now host to cultural events and a garden bistro. *Piazza Velasca 5*

Torre Branca

Next door to the Triennale museum (see p026), Torre Branca is an elegant metal structure that looms 108m above Parco Sempione. It was designed by Gio Ponti with Cesare Chiodi and Ettore Ferrari in 1933 for the fifth Triennale (exhibitions were previously held once every three years, hence the name). For €5 you can ride up to the viewing platform, though you'll need a head for heights and a fair degree of patience, since the lift can only hold a small group at a time, who must descend before the next one is allowed up. Opening hours are erratic, so call ahead: it's worth the hassle for such a rewarding panorama. Afterwards, calm the nerves with a stroll through the art-strewn lawns and halls of design in the Triennale. *Viale Luigi Camoens 2, Parco Sempione, T 02 331 4120*

Pirelli Tower

This iconic skyscraper near the Stazione Centrale is proof positive that a modernist high-rise need not result in repetitive banality. Constructed for tyre giant Pirelli and completed in 1958, it was the tallest building in the country, at 127m, until it was overshadowed by Pei Cobb Freed & Partners' Palazzo Lombardia (see p009) in 2010. Its architect, Gio Ponti, was joined by several collaborators on the project,

including engineer Pier Luigi Nervi, and the design helped shape Ponti's career. In 1978, unable to meet the huge running costs, Pirelli sold the complex to the local government, which relocated to Palazzo Lombardia in 2011 but retains office space here. Il Pirellone, as it is fondly known by locals, was entirely refurbished after an aircraft famously flew into it in 2002.
Piazza Duca d'Aosta 3

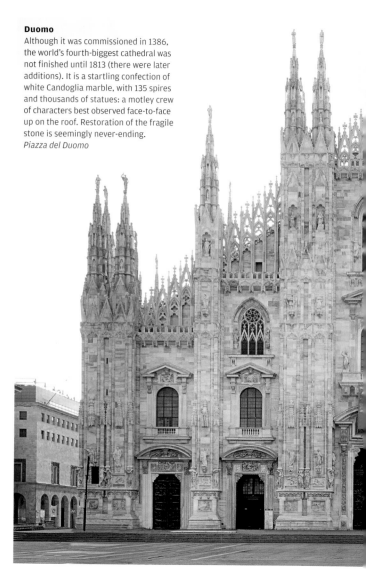

Duomo

Although it was commissioned in 1386, the world's fourth-biggest cathedral was not finished until 1813 (there were later additions). It is a startling confection of white Candoglia marble, with 135 spires and thousands of statues: a motley crew of characters best observed face-to-face up on the roof. Restoration of the fragile stone is seemingly never-ending.
Piazza del Duomo

HOTELS

WHERE TO STAY AND WHICH ROOMS TO BOOK

Since the spotlight of the 2015 Expo, the city has developed into a genuine tourist destination, and a slew of hotels has sprung up to add to the existing gems that were tuned to the frequencies of its fashion and design industries. Setting the standard in the boutique category are the eminently à la mode Senato (see p018); slick Viu (see p020); Palazzo Segreti (see p022), furnished like a series of intimate apartments; and eccentric The Yard (see p023). These join the soft-brutalist Straf (Via San Raffaele 3, T 02 805 081), designed by Vincenzo De Cotiis (see p062), and industrial-chic Magna Pars Suites (Via Forcella 6, T 02 833 8371), which is set in an old perfume factory with a Pompidou-esque facade and a central garden.

Two Milan classics are the Bulgari (opposite), which occupies a modernist block within the gardens of an old monastery, and the Armani Hotel (Via Manzoni 31, T 02 8883 8888), a realisation of the fashion designer's aesthetic inside Enrico A Griffini's rationalist 1937 building, with a sleek spa and infinity pool in its glass 'hat' that has an unbeatable panorama. For a more traditional getaway, the Four Seasons (Via Gesù 6-8, T 02 77 088) encompasses a 15th-century convent and a 17th-century palazzo, encircling a courtyard, while Palazzo Parigi (Corso di Porto Nuova 1, T 02 625 625), though new, is neoclassically styled with a balcony for each room. Even if you are not a guest, drop by either for high tea in the conservatory or garden. *For full addresses and room rates, see Resources.*

Bulgari Hotel

The luxe accessory brand's first hotel was created in 2004 by Antonio Citterio, and renovated for its 10th anniversary. The 58 rooms, including 11 suites (Premium 416, above), are dominated by oak, bronze and black marble, and most have views of the 4,000 sq m gardens that were first tended by monks 300 years ago, offering a retreat from the bustle of the Quadrilatero della Moda. The exceptional spa incorporates a gold mosaic pool, a Turkish bath set in an emerald-glass cube, an external jacuzzi and a couples' treatment area. All rooms feature Citterio's total design, in the wood panelling, teak furnishings and travertine bathrooms; our favourite is the penthouse Bulgari Suite for its wraparound balcony. In summer, the patio bar is a real hotspot.
Via Privata Fratelli Gabba 7b,
T 02 805 8051, www.bulgarihotels.com

Senato Hotel

The intimate Senato was converted from a late 19th-century townhouse by Alessandro Bianchi and retains quite a dash. The hotel symbol is the ginkgo leaf (an art nouveau motif), and it appears as a profusion of sconces in reception, handcrafted in brass by Bottega Gadda. The firm also executed Bianchi's lamp cluster and desk in the café (above) and the circular furniture in the lobby, which has a marble floor pattern referencing the Visconti snake. The floral curation is by Rosalba Piccinni (see p036), and Cristina Celestino (see p067) created the candleholders. The 43 whitewashed rooms have Carrara-clad bathrooms and oak floors; Junior Suites boast a terrace. The decorative courtyard pool (opposite) evokes the canal that once ran past outside.
Via Senato 22, T 02 781 236,
www.senatohotelmilano.it

Hotel Viu
The big draw at this purpose-built hotel, opened in 2017, is the heated pool on the rooftop. The seven-storey glass block by architects Arassociati is bookended with vertical gardens. Nicola Gallizia kitted it out with low-slung furnishings, parquet floors, basalt tiling and Rubelli textiles. Out of the 124 rooms, the standout is Viu Suite 701 (pictured) for its two balconies.
Via Fioravanti 6, T 02 8001 0910

Palazzo Segreti

On a tranquil street near the 15th-century Castello Sforzesco, Palazzo Segreti lives up to its name as something of a hidden spot. Inside a late 19th-century townhouse, the pared-back scheme was conceived by owners Roberta and Francesco Tibaldi with architects Brizzi+Riefenstahl. Exposed brick and concrete are juxtaposed with darkwood floors and modern furnishings in the lobby as well as in the 18 distinct rooms, each of which exudes a sense of intimacy. The Unique Suite and two Junior Design Suites (Room 8, above) have large freestanding tubs near the beds. Breakfast is a fine spread of regional organic produce (a pleasant change from sugary brioche). In the evenings, charcuterie, local cheese and Italian wines are served in the lounge. *Via San Tomaso 8, T 02 4952 9250, www.palazzosegreti.com*

The Yard

This sprawling property is festooned with an eccentric collection of antique sports memorabilia and dandy accoutrements. The overstuffed leather armchairs, worn barber chairs, cane stands of polo mallets and oars, and shelves of riding boots give it a real gentleman's club vibe. A warren of lounges and studies lead to the amusingly named Doping Club (above), modelled on an apothecary; there's a pizzeria done up like a boxing gym, behind which is a tiny 'secret' bar; a tapas restaurant (in honour of the sister location in Ibiza), which puts on live music; and a cinema. The 32 kooky rooms are strewn with books and athletic gear and feel like private residences; the Maison Wicket has its own 1930s bar, and is perfect for hosting an intimate soirée. *Piazza XXIV Maggio 8, T 02 8941 5901, www.theyardmilano.com*

24 HOURS

SEE THE BEST OF THE CITY IN JUST ONE DAY

Make the city's unparalleled design culture the focus of your day. Kick off with a light breakfast at Pasticceria Marchesi (opposite), then tour the Triennale (see p026) before lunch with views from its top floor. In the afternoon, make for the expansive galleries at Fondazione Prada (see p028), which also has a beautiful cinema and the wonderland of Wes Anderson's café (see p044). Or spend a few hours in a former workshop or villa of one of Milan's famous sons, at Fondazione Piero Portaluppi (Via Morozzo della Rocca 5, T 02 3652 1591), Vico Magistretti (see p066) or Studio Museo Achille Castiglioni (see p069). For an insight into the wealth and lifestyle of the early industrialists, peruse Villa Necchi Campiglio (see p029).

Now it is time for that most Milanese part of the day, aperitivo. Dry (see p043) serves an invigorating French 75, or head to Navigli for a *passeggiata* along the canal, which is lined with bars; nearby Carlo e Camilla (see p030) is our pick for cocktails. Afterwards, if you want a quick bite, drop by Pescaria (Via Nino Bonnet 5, T 02 659 9322) for fast fish, raw and fried. Or dine in style at Innocenti Evasioni (Via Privata della Bindellina, T 02 3300 1882), which has a beautiful garden setting, or Lume (Via Giacomo Watt, T 02 8088 8624), installed in the former Richard Ginori factory. Alternatively, there's quite a scene developing in Porta Romana, spearheaded by hip Dabass (see p031) and neighbouring The Spirit (see p052). *For full addresses, see Resources.*

08.30 Pasticceria Marchesi

With walls of minty Venetian plaster part-covered with a floral silk-jacquard fabric, green velvet chairs and deep-hued Alpine marble floors and tables, Marchesi's third outpost, in Galleria Vittorio Emanuele II, is an almost mind-bending interpretation of *pasticceria* pastels. Its tearoom (where cocktails are served in the evening) evokes a fantastical garden, and is piled high with candy-coloured cakes. Roberto Baciocchi's design riffs on the interior of the 1824 shop on Via S Maria alla Porta (T 02 862 770). Since 2014, it has been owned by Prada; drop in before visiting the label's museum-like store below, its first, dating from 1913, and the Prada Foundation's Osservatorio (T 02 5666 2611), which shows photography and has superlative views of the Duomo. *Galleria Vittorio Emanuele II, T 02 9418 1710, www.pasticceriamarchesi.com*

10.30 Triennale di Milano

Reminiscent of classical architecture with its tall slim arches, Giovanni Muzio's 1933 rationalist building, constructed to host Italy's early expos, became the country's first design museum in 2007. Its extensive collection ranges from the pure functional beauty of Sottsass' typewriters for Olivetti to Gio Ponti's rule-breaking prototypes, and temporary shows are often sweeping overviews that incorporate architecture, fashion, photography and contemporary art. The sculpture garden features Gaetano Pesce's 'UP5' chair in bronze, and Giorgio de Chirico's *Bagni Misteriosi* fountain, the café is furnished with emblematic chairs, and the rooftop osteria (opposite), a glass pavilion devised by architects OBR, merits a visit on its own, especially on a clear day. *Viale Alemagna 6, T 02 724 341, www.triennale.org*

14.00 Fondazione Prada

Housed in a 1910 gin distillery transformed by OMA's Rem Koolhaas, Miuccia Prada's gallery is double the size of the Whitney. It displays contemporary art from her own collection, and rotating projects in hangar-like expanses and hallways. Some silos and warehouses remain raw; others have been reinterpreted in mirrored glass and shiny metals, such as the four-storey 'Haunted House' (above), clad in 24-carat gold leaf, which hosts a Robert Gober installation and two works by Louise Bourgeois. Elsewhere you'll find pieces by Barnett Newman, Jeff Koons and Donald Judd, and Italian shows have included Francesco Vezzoli's study of 1970s TV. A 60m-tall white concrete tower, replete with a restaurant and observation deck, was added in 2018. Closed Tuesdays. *Largo Isarco 2, T 02 5666 2611, www.fondazioneprada.org*

16.30 Villa Necchi Campiglio

Immortalised in Luca Guadagnino's 2009 film *I Am Love*, this rationalist villa offers a rare glimpse into the private world of Milan's great industrialists. The owners were sisters Gigina and Nedda Necchi, and Gigina's husband, Angelo Campiglio. Manufacturers of sewing machines and refrigerator motors from the 1920s to the 1960s, the family was renowned for its chic parties. The villa was designed by local architect Piero Portaluppi and constructed between 1932 and 1935; it was converted into a museum in 2008. The interiors are a sumptuous combination of marble, fine woods and antiques, and part of Claudia Gian Ferrari's vast collection of early 20th-century art is displayed throughout. Open Wednesdays to Sundays, 10am to 6pm. *Via Mozart 14, T 02 7634 0121, www.villanecchicampiglio.it*

19.00 Carlo e Camilla in Segheria

Tanja Solci masterminded the conversion of this 1932 sawmill belonging to her father (Carlo). The shell has been kept bare, with exposed steel and brick, cement walls, and a high, slanted roof, from which hang antique chandeliers. Two long communal tables intersect and are set out as if for a banquet, laid with porcelain tableware by Richard Ginori. Chef Luca Pedata's refined Emilia-Romagna and Neapolitan menu features a signature dish of cannoli filled with Parmesan cream on raw mince with ragù and nutmeg. The majolica-tiled bar just off the main space serves cocktails such as Sexy Peaches, which incorporates vodka, wine, celery, tarragon, verbena and tamarillo, and the patio courtyard is most convivial for aperitivo on a warm evening. *Via Giuseppe Meda 24, T 02 837 3963, www.carloecamillainsegheria.it*

21.30 Dabass

In a wedge-shaped art nouveau palazzo, a hotchpotch of fleamarket chairs, vintage plates and a ceramic counter installation by Graziano Locatelli lend lo-fi Dabass a cosy informality – yet it's at the forefront of a culinary renaissance. Andrea Marroni uses seasonal produce and contemporary techniques, like sous vide and elements of molecular gastronomy, to create a tasting menu of four tapas-like servings that might include poached egg with saffron risotto cream and a pork cheek wafer, or paccheri with cheese and pepper, *coratella* (lamb offal) and artichoke. There are also larger plates such as barbecued guinea fowl and ox rib, as well as homemade focaccia and house-cured charcuterie. Equally inventive are the cocktails and selection of organic and natural wines from small producers.
Via Piacenza 13, T 02 4537 1120

URBAN LIFE

CAFÉS, RESTAURANTS, BARS AND NIGHTCLUBS

Post-Expo, the city is hitting top speed, and excellent dining options abound. Ritzy openings have won Michelin stars and respect for the gastro scene, among them Matias Perdomo's playfully imaginative Contraste (Via Meda 2, T 02 4953 6597); Seta (Via Andegari 9, T 02 8731 8897), where Antonio Guida's menu is served in a palatial courtyard; and Enrico Bartolini (Mudec, Via Tortona 56, T 02 8429 3701), which melds tradition and innovation. Other spots buzz with concepts that would never have taken off here not so long ago: the restaurant/club mash-up at Apollo (see p034), more multitasking at design gallery/bistro Six (see p048), and even Peruvian cuisine (no pasta?) at Pacifico (see p040). There is a panoply of distinctive venues in which to take your aperitivo too, from Carlo e Camilla (see p030) to The Botanical Club (see p041), Bottiglieria Spartaco (see p046) and the al fresco bar at the 1937 pool Bagni Misteriosi (Via Carlo Botta 18, T 02 8973 1800), now restored to its full glory.

Plenty of things don't need changing, however – this is Italy, after all. Classic haunts invoke undying affection from locals, who favour spritzes at Bar Basso (Via Plinio 39, T 02 2940 0580), the birthplace of the negroni *sbagliato*, and veal cutlets at Trattoria Masuelli San Marco (Viale Umbria 80, T 02 5518 4138). Of course, decent coffee is easy to find; just don't ask for a cappuccino after 12pm (it's strictly macchiato or caffè post-noon) if you want to avoid the sneers. *For full addresses, see Resources.*

L'Arabesque

In a 1949 block by architect Paolo Buffa, L'Arabesque comprises restaurant L'île (above), a café, a bookshop and boutiques for menswear, womenswear and vintage, as well as accessories and fragrance, with midcentury furniture throughout, all of which is for sale. Owner Chichi Meroni lives upstairs, creating elaborate fashion inspired by pieces from the 1920s to the 1970s. The café chimes with the overall aesthetic, done out with wavy rubber flooring by Gio Ponti and 'Bubble' lights by George Nelson; dishes sometimes show a retro touch too. To drink, there is a list of classic cocktails and a fine selection of Lombardy wines – try the sparkling white from Oltrepò Pavese or a Valtellina red. It stays open until 10pm; closed Sundays.
Largo Augusto 10, Via Francesco Sforza 4, T 02 7634 1477, www.larabesque.net

Apollo Milano

Colonising an old factory, this multivalent enterprise — designed by Apollo founders Marcellina Di Chio and Tiberio Carcano, together with UAO Studio — is a lot of fun. The restaurant (above), which serves global and Italian fare like rosemary-smoked sea bream with cannellini and beetroot cream, and games room (opposite) are appointed in jewel-toned furnishings from the 1930s to the 1950s; there are candelabras and antiques, swathes of velvet and potted palms. There is also a separate cocktail bar, but the real highlight here is Friday's long-running disco-house party Rollover in the adjacent club space. On other nights there might be live music or DJs, and on Sundays there's brunch followed by a film screening. Closed Mondays and Tuesdays. *Via Giosuè Borsi 9, T 02 8942 0969, www.apollomilano.com*

Potafiori

A café/bistro/cocktail bar that doubles as a florist, Potafiori has scored an ace with its unlikely formula. Storage Associati has devised a pared-back look, and the neutral colours contrast with the floral explosions seen on every surface. Huge slabs of Ceppo Lombardo limestone form long benches, a buffet bar, and a watering fountain with brass pipes. Head chef Giorgio Bresciani prepares regional Italian dishes, such as Culatello di Zibello ham with goat's cheese and figs, and paccheri pasta with black and purple aubergines and clams. Inventive cocktails include the Timoepepe, a mix of smoked vodka, Cointreau, lemon, thyme and chilli. Owner Rosalba Piccinni, a jazz singer, is known for breaking into song, a pal taking to the piano, at aperitivo hour. *17 Via Salasco, T 02 8706 5930, www.potafiori.com*

T'a Milano Restaurant & Bistro

Brothers Tancredi and Alberto, scions of the Alemagna baking family, launched their own artisan chocolatier in 2008. This flagship arrived eight years later inside an ornate neoclassical building, with a smart, opulent interior by Vincenzo De Cotiis (see p062), featuring his Progetto Domestico 'DC115A' chairs, mobile-style chandeliers, Kvadrat velvet banquettes, and floors of swirling marble. Lunch and dinner menus include a few experimental dishes, like the tortelli filled with orange-infused ricotta, sautéed cacio cheese, pepper and cacao. But the artistry works best in the desserts and handmade chocolates, displayed at the counter. The aperitivo offering is also a hit – try the signature Pink Momo cocktail (gin, violet liqueur and syrup, and lime). *Via Clerici 1, T 02 8738 6130, www.tamilano.com*

Ceresio 7

On top of the 1930s Enel Building, Ceresio 7 was launched in 2013 by Dean and Dan Caten, with help from Storage Associati. In summer it draws an impeccably turned-out crowd to two outdoor pools flanked by cabanas and terraces with wraparound views (above). The bar and restaurant, in which Dimore Studio's interiors nod to the building's rationalist heritage, open until 1am. Amid the vintage and contemporary furniture, velvet and brass, are decorative elements, such as a Gio Ponti tea set. Chef Elio Sironi often uses the grill or the wood oven, and adds a twist to the classics, like the carbonara spaghetti with turmeric and scallops, or the Vignola cherries in spiced red wine and chocolate. There's a sleek spa downstairs, also designed by Storage. *Via Ceresio 7, T 02 3103 9221, www.ceresio7.com*

Pacifico

Marsica Fossati's interior for this Peruvian-Nikkei restaurant is all oceanic escapism. You'll find a palette of deep blues, marine motifs, porthole-shaped mirrors, 'Jardin d'Osier' wallpaper from Hermès (above), velvet stools, brass light fixtures by local studio Servomuto, and Hokusai-inspired washrooms. It is headlined by chef Jaime Pesaque, acclaimed for his Mayta in Lima; here Ernesto Espinoza leads the kitchen, sending out dainty ceviches, *tiraditos* and *anticuchos*, with veal tataki a highlight, as well as moreish seafood dishes. Seating 20, the Submarine Room has a well-stocked bar and a club-worthy sound system, and often hosts kicking parties. The cocktail list is awash with pisco: try a NonCaPisco, with ginger beer, grapefruit and Campari. *Via San Marco/Via della Moscova, T 02 8724 4737, www.wearepacifico.it*

The Botanical Club

The original Botanical Club (T 02 3652 3846), a gin distillery, bar and restaurant, was an instant hit in 2015, and helped to transform a scruffy corner of Isola. A year on, it launched this second, larger venue, specialising in artisanal gin, and cocktails prepared using small-batch liquors and house-made infusions. There's a menu of creative takes on Italian dishes like wild boar meatballs and creamed cod, plus a raw bar and poké bowls. It is flooded with light in the day, with sharp-angled wrought-iron fixtures, darkwood floors and a mass of greenery. The team has branched out with Champagne Socialist (T 02 204 7295), a natural wine bar/store with 500 labels from boutique vineyards around Italy and Europe, and tastings on Saturdays at noon.
Via Tortona 33, T 02 423 2890,
www.thebotanicalclub.com

Otto

Since it was pedestrianised in 2014, Via Paolo Sarpi in Chinatown has become a pleasant and heterogeneous enclave, and unpretentious all-day hangout Otto has injected a hip, youthful vibe. It's a tranquil, plant-strewn oasis, filled with a mishmash of salvaged chairs and communal tables that lend it a living-room feel, and there's an expansive terrace. A signature is the *quadrotti* – open sandwiches topped with healthy, unusual combos, such as avocado cream, feta, cucumber, mint and toasted seeds. At weekends, these are incorporated into a brunch accompanied by four sides, perhaps carrots with turmeric, or hummus, presented on a wooden board. Or come at night for inventive cocktails like the Anna (prosecco, basil and berries) and Haruna (horseradish vodka, lemon and vanilla).
Via Paolo Sarpi 8, www.sarpiotto.com

Dry Milano

The owners of next-door bistro Pisacco (T 02 9176 5472) have struck gold with this superior pizza-and-cocktails concept, initially dreamt up by chef Andrea Berton (see p099). Vudafieri Saverino Partners gave Dry an industrial edge with plenty of brass, mirrors and exposed bulbs. Videos are projected onto the walls as part of a collaboration with Paola Clerico's project CaseChiuse, which showcases young local artists. From the kitchen, try the calzone filled with baked olives, anchovy butter and smoked provola, accompanied by a negroni mixed with aged Campari. This original location is only open for dinner; a glossy second outpost in Porta Venezia (T 02 6347 1564) also offers a pared-down lunch menu as well as outdoor seating. *Via Solferino 33, T 02 6379 3414, www.drymilano.it*

Bar Luce
Within Fondazione Prada (see p028), Bar
Luce is old-school café life envisioned by
film director Wes Anderson, who designed
not just the interior but every single detail,
including the sugar packets. His whimsical
tableau pays homage to Galleria Vittorio
Emanuele II, in the wallpaper above the
veneered wood panels and a ceiling that
evokes its atrium. The Formica furniture
in lurid pastels, swing trays, terrazzo floor
and spherical pendant lights allude to the
1960s, a hot pink jukebox plays the Italian
crooners (naturally) and a pair of seafoam-
green pinball machines feature Anderson
films. It serves pastries and panini (the
tonno scatenato packs in tuna, cannellini
beans, Tropea onion and robiola cheese),
and cocktails like the Aperitivo Luce (gin,
Campari, Chambord, Oscar 697 extra-dry
vermouth and cardamom), which also tend
to come in full colour. Closed Tuesdays.
Largo Isarco 2, T 02 5666 2611,
www.fondazioneprada.org/barluce

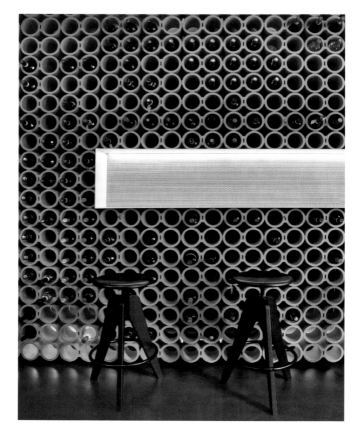

Bottiglieria Spartaco

Kooky and diminutive Bottiglieria Spartaco has a wonderful variety of wines and sakes chosen by Japanese owner Norie Harada, who spent a decade as a sommelier at Joël Robuchon and Alain Ducasse. Designed by Francesco Rota, the bar features low-rise 'Tommy' stools by Sipa and a feature wall of cotto, traditionally used for bottle racks. Trust Harada's well-honed picks – perhaps the 2011 Barbaresco reserve from Cuneo in Piemonte, or the Selve Picotendro from the Aosta Valley, aged in chestnut barrels. Signature sakes include the dry Tenzan, from the Saga region, and the smoother Garyubai, from Shizuoka. Pair them with her eclectic small plates, such as tofu with olive oil and white truffle, caviar with sour cream or anchovies on toast. It fills up fast with local fashion-industry professionals. *Via Spartaco 11, T 02 8456 8911*

Orsonero

European and US coffee culture has barely impacted Italy, where a takeaway order can still mean a china demitasse and saucer covered with foil, to be returned on your honour. Canadian Brent Jopson and his Milanese wife, Giulia Gasperini, introduced the city to modern concepts at Orsonero in 2016, and serve a rotating selection of single-origin filter coffees from small-batch roasters here and abroad, and espresso from Gardelli in Emilia-Romagna, made on a La Marzocco Strada machine. There are also quality teas, pastries, cakes and Italian craft beers. Designed by local architects Forestieri Pace Pezzani, the cosy venue is stylishly fitted out in fir and okoume wood. A granular concrete floor unifies indoors and outdoors, and a full-wall letterboard behind the low counter displays the menu. *Via Broggi 15, T 366 547 7441*

Six

This upscale complex opened in 2017, and encompasses bistro Sixième, design store Six, and green boutique Irene – hence the oversized plants – set around a courtyard. Originally a 16th-century monastery, and later communal flats, it was reimagined by architects Quincoces-Dragò, who stripped back layers of plaster to reveal the original bricks and floors. Under a glass roof, the gallery (opposite) displays vintage pieces such as Gabriella Crespi's 'Square Table', as well as contemporary works by glass artist Yali and others. The sceney dining room/bar (above), lit by Isamu Noguchi pendant lamps, serves intriguing dishes like Wagyu *trippa* with chickpeas and cinnamon, and drinks include the Mombasa (rye whiskey, banana liqueur and coffee). Closed Sunday. *Via Scaldasole 7, T 02 3651 9910, www.sixieme-bistro.com*

Il Liberty

Pocket-sized Il Liberty has built up a loyal following owing to the flair of chef Andrea Provenzani, who reinterprets northern Italian cuisine using influences from Peru, Japan, Thailand and Mexico. Come here for artful dishes such as calamari with broad beans and chicory, or spaghetti with citrus and sea urchin pesto; and ingredients rare in Milanese cooking, including ginger, fresh turmeric and avocado. Tasting menus of up to seven courses might end with a crisp cylinder of chocolate cream smoked with pipe tobacco with fior di latte ice cream, or crème brûlée with berries, followed by a signature G&T. A renovation by Carlo Donati Studio deployed exposed brick, duck-egg-blue walls, burnished brass, amber glass, wrought iron and panels of Liberty print. *Viale Monte Grappa 6, T 02 2901 1439, www.il-liberty.it*

Erba Brusca

Located in an idyllic spot to the south of the city centre, this bright and breezy restaurant was designed by Milan-based Rgastudio, who channelled the spirit of the venue's canalside setting to create the interior. Owner Alice Delcourt was born in France and raised in the US; she honed her skills at River Café in London and Il Liberty (opposite) before opening Erba Brusca in 2011. The kitchen garden lends it a bucolic aspect, yet the ambience feels cosmopolitan. Homegrown produce features year-round, from the asparagus to go with egg salad, thyme breadcrumbs and hollandaise sauce, to the mushrooms destined for soup with sourdough crostini. It's open Wednesdays to Sundays. You can hire wheels here to cycle along the canal.
Alzaia Naviglio Pavese 286, T 02 8738 0711, www.erbabrusca.it

The Spirit

Hidden away next to Dabass (see p031), behind a heavy, metal-studded door, this plush, colourful bar is lined with golden shelves of rare liquors, labels and libations. Venezuelan designer Juan Carlos Viso has imbued references to art nouveau and art deco with a sense of alchemy – curios and objets d'art relate to astrology, time travel and tarot. Velvet and leather furnishings come in peacock blue, emerald, mustard and ruby, and the mahogany bar is inlaid with onyx. The 15 to 20 house cocktails are also inspired by fantasy, often smoked or featuring obscure ingredients (poitín, umeshu, Herbsaint) in concoctions such as The Poisoned Arrow (Pays d'Auge Calvados Dupont, créme de poire, lemon, grenadine, apple juice). Or stay honest with a limited-edition Macchu Pisco, or Don Q's Reserva de la Familia Serrallés, a 20-year-old rum.
Via Piacenza 15, T 02 8457 0612, www.thespirit.it

INSIDERS' GUIDE

SIMONE RIZZO AND LORIS MESSINA, FASHION DESIGNERS

Calabrian Simone Rizzo (left) and Loris Messina, from Grenoble, moved to Milan and set up cult label Sunnei (see p090) in 2013. 'The quality of life here is so high,' says Rizzo. 'You eat well, see beautiful things, and can still work. We wouldn't live in any other place.' On days off, they often seek inspiration at Converso (Piazza Sant'Eufemia, T 02 866 247), a deconsecrated church that hosts occasional installations, HangarBicocca (see p064) or Lia Rumma (see p071), but are equally likely to cycle over to the Duomo (see p014) 'to watch people in knock-offs taking selfies with pigeons. This tourist influx is a new thing and we're fascinated by it'.

They might wrap up a day at work with a drink at Champagne Socialist (see p041) or Bar Basso (see p032), and favourite eateries include Japanese canteen Gastronomia Yamamoto (Via Amedei 5, T 02 3674 1426), Carnivore Union (Viale Nazario Sauro 5, T 327 777 4904), for Chinese hot pot cooked and served at long communal tables, and 'tiny but perfect' Lile in Cucina (Via Guicciardini 5, T 02 4963 2629), which proposes new twists on Italian dishes in a cosy setting. They recommend visitors head to Santa Marta Suites (Via Santa Marta 4, T 02 4537 3369) to dine on the top-floor terrace.

'In Milan, it's aperitivo, dinner, and then ciao! Nightlife is not a big thing,' adds Rizzo. But when they do venture out dancing, it is to the parties at Dude Club (Via Boncompagni 44, T 392 236 8752). *For full addresses, see Resources.*

ART AND DESIGN
GALLERIES, STUDIOS AND PUBLIC SPACES

Salone del Mobile casts the spotlight on Milan, but it dazzles all year round thanks to a surfeit of locally based talent that helps maintain the potency of the 'Made in Italy' label. The nexus of the furniture industry is Brianza, where the great masters developed their ideas in collaboration with highly skilled manufacturers and artisans, a process brought to life in the city's studio museums (see p024). The work of today's generation is on display in galleries such as Dimore (see p060) and Luisa delle Piane (see p063).

A flourishing art scene is best experienced at Kaufmann Repetto (see p059), Lia Rumma (see p071) and Massimo de Carlo (Piazza Belgioioso 2, T 02 3663 6990), which launched in the creative hub of Lambrate and has expanded into an 18th-century mansion. The civic focus has long been on the Renaissance – see the fresco-laden San Maurizio al Monastero Maggiore (Corso Magenta 15, T 02 8844 5208) and the Pinacoteca di Brera (Via Brera 28, T 02 7226 3264), although it is spreading into Palazzo Citterio (see p072) in 2019, in order to show modern work. But it is commercial largesse that has given this industrial city the contemporary institutions it deserves. Pirelli's behemoth HangarBicocca (see p064) has been joined by Gallerie d'Italia (Piazza della Scala 6, T 800 167 619), a neoclassical palazzo filled with Intesa Sanpaolo's extensive art collection, and the vast, game-changing Fondazione Prada (see p028).

For full addresses, see Resources.

Chiesa di Santa Maria Annunciata

US artist Dan Flavin completed the plans for this, his untitled final work, just days before his death in 1996. The installation of blue, green, red and gold neon within the church of Santa Maria Annunciata in Chiesa Rossa was facilitated with the help of New York's Dia Art Foundation and the Fondazione Prada (see p028), which commissioned the piece. The church itself is a 1932 creation by the prolific Giovanni Muzio, and was designed in the classical style of purified grandeur that had found favour during the fascist era. Flavin always rejected spiritual readings of his abstract compositions, but the transcendental overtones of this sublimely serene work seem to reflect a more mystical vision at the end of his life. It's best viewed at dusk.
Via Neera 24,
www.parrocchiachiesarossa.net

LOVE

Artist Maurizio Cattelan is perhaps Milan's most mischievous son. In 2010, he unveiled a sculpture of a 4.7m-tall hand, beautifully carved in traditional Carrara marble, with only the middle finger remaining. Cattelan has called it a commentary on the fascist salute and a criticism of totalitarianism but its placement in front of the 1932 Palazzo Mezzanotte stock exchange invites a more contemporary reading. Just as Wall Street's charging bull is a symbol of the optimism of its era, the sculpture has come to embody a distrust of the financial establishment, but it is ambiguous whether the gesture is directed at the bankers or if it portrays the industry's own disregard of the world. Its deceptive title, *LOVE*, is an acronym for freedom, hate, revenge, eternity – locals simply refer to it as *Il Dito* (The Finger). *Piazza degli Affari*

Kaufmann Repetto

In 2010, this eclectic gallery run by sisters Francesca Kaufmann and Chiara Repetto relocated to a more spacious concrete-floored space designed by Frank Boehm beside Parco Sempione. It has been on a roll ever since. A project room is dedicated to experimental work, with everything from multimedia and performance art to photography and painting, and outdoor sculptures are displayed in the courtyard.

It's admired for exhibiting fresh, compelling pieces by artists including Eva Rothschild, Pae White, Adrian Paci and Thea Djordjadze ('Oxymoron Grey', above), as well as for championing new talent. Nearby, Otto (see p042) and Cantine Isola (T 02 331 5249), an enoteca since 1896, are both superior options for a post-show glass of wine. *Via di Porta Tenaglia 7, T 02 7209 4331, www.kaufmannrepetto.com*

Dimore Gallery

Milanese duo Britt Moran and Emiliano Salci established Dimore Gallery in 2014. A warren of rooms within an 18th-century palazzo display their own lavish creations and vintage classics by the likes of Gabriella Crespi. For instance, their 'Lampada 092' floor light, with its curving chrome arms supporting a trio of spherical glass shades (the top half tinted) stands over a walnut veneer sideboard by Osvaldo Borsani and a coffee table by Gio Ponti (all opposite). Elsewhere, their rounded 'Matera' table shares space with Luigi Caccia Dominioni's pendant lamps for Azucena (above). You'll also find their textile line, Progetto Tessuti, and work by young locally based designers, such as Ilaria Bianchi, who crafts furniture and bookcases from cast-off materials. *Via Solferino 11, T 02 3656 3420, www.dimoregallery.com*

De Cotiis Gallery

You may well first encounter architect and designer Vincenzo De Cotiis' reconstructed, reappropriated, sculptural aesthetic in the Straf hotel (see p016), T'a café (see p037) or fashion store Antonia (see p088). In his search for 'perfect imperfection', De Cotiis creates either one-offs or limited editions, seamlessly melding low and high materials, such as fibreglass salvaged from boat hulls or recycled leather, juxtaposed with shiny metal, translucent resin or smooth polished marble. All his work celebrates patina, and is as tactile as it is visual. Striking pieces such as the 'DC1727' wall cabinet and the 'DC1717' coffee table (above) from the 2017 Baroquisme collection, which incorporate Murano glass and silvered cast brass, are offset by the minimalism of his showroom. *Via Carlo de Cristoforis 14, T 02 8728 7757, www.decotiis.it*

Luisa delle Piane

One of the city's most respected figures, Luisa delle Piane has collected and sold furniture, design, art and jewellery since the 1970s. Her multi-roomed Chinatown gallery, which opened way back in 1994, displays everything from Gabetti, Isola and Drocco's glass-topped 'Trilogy' table, with curved chrome legs, to a Gaetano Pesce leather print and Christoph Radl's text-based monochrome wallpaper (all above). Alongside pieces by midcentury Italian heavy-hitters – Franco Albini, Gio Ponti, Ico Parisi, Ettore Sottsass – there are contemporary Milanese makers too. Look out for minimalist work by new-wave carpenter Giacomo Moor, and quirky wood seating by Mario Ceroli, beside geometric neon lamps by Venetian Giorgia Zanellato. *Via Giusti 24, T 02 331 9680, www.gallerialuisadellepiane.it*

Pirelli HangarBicocca

The north-eastern industrial district of Bicocca was occupied by the vast Pirelli complex until the mid-1980s, when the company began one of Europe's most ambitious regeneration projects. The area now accommodates multinationals, a university, student dorms and, since 2004, HangarBicocca, a contemporary art museum set in and around a former train-parts factory. It is home to large-scale installations including *La Sequenza* (pictured) by Fausto Melotti, inspired by ancient Greek architecture, Bach's music and paintings by Piero della Francesca; and Anselm Kiefer's huge, haunting *The Seven Heavenly Palaces*; and puts on four provocative shows a year by big names. Open Thursday to Sunday, 10am to 10pm. *Via Chiese 2, T 02 6611 1573, www.hangarbicocca.org*

Fondazione Vico Magistretti

Milan born and bred, Vico Magistretti had a major influence on 20th-century Italian aesthetics. During the 1940s and 1950s, he contributed to the experimental district QT8 in the city suburbs, as well as an estate for Pirelli workers. In product design, he focused on functional furniture that could be mass produced, creating classics such as the 'Carimate' chair for Cassina. Visit the studio where he worked for 60 years to peruse his extraordinary archive. The foundation also suggests itineraries for an excursion to 14 of Magistretti's buildings, as well as a tour of the showrooms of firms affiliated with his work (Artemide, Flou, De Padova and Schiffini). Open Tuesday (10am to 6pm), Thursday (2pm to 8pm) and the last Saturday of the month (11am to 3pm). *Via Conservatorio 20, T 02 7600 2964, www.vicomagistretti.it*

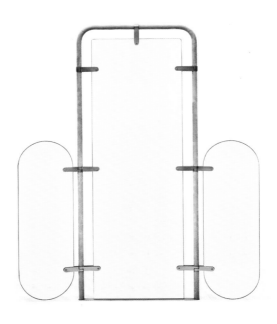

Cristina Celestino

Trained as an architect, Cristina Celestino set up her Milan studio in 2010, creating furniture, lighting, glassware and home accessories with a whimsical retro charm. Commissions for brands including Nilufar (see p081) have included a velvet and fox-fur sofa for Fendi's glam installation 'The Happy Room'; tassel-trimmed 'Madama' pendant lights for Mogg; and 'Calatea', a leaf-inspired chair for Pianca. A fit-out for Sergio Rossi's Paris store, later imported to Via Montenapoleone (T 02 7600 6140), included 'Icona' (above), a tri-fold mirror with copper 'pincers'. Her Attico Design brand puts out covetable pieces like the 'Atomizer' condiment dispensers, part of the collection at the Triennale (see p026), and the 'Gemmazione' platters in speckled glass. Studio visits by appointment only. *www.cristinacelestino.com*

Memphis | Post Design Gallery

Spread throughout six rooms, in changing displays, Post Design exhibits and sells the work of the riotous, era-defining Memphis group. Ettore Sottsass formed the po-mo movement in Milan in 1981 with Michele De Lucchi, Matteo Thun, George Sowden, Nathalie Du Pasquier et al, using cheap new materials, vivid tones and no little wit to reject Bauhaus functionalism; his graphic, multicoloured 'Carlton' room divider says it all, even in miniature (above, top centre). Also on show are the two Meta Memphis collections, from 1989 and 1991, by artists including Alighiero Boetti and Michelangelo Pistoletto, beside contemporary pieces by young guns like Giacomo Moor. Much of it is eminently portable; we picked up Martine Bedin's 'Super' lamp (above, foreground). *Largo Treves 5, T 02 655 4731, www.memphis-milano.com*

Studio Museo Achille Castiglioni

The studio in which the legendary Achille Castiglioni worked for 40 years until his death in 2002 was remodelled into this museum, opened in 2006. It provides a unique insight into the outstanding career and rich legacy of one of Italy's most highly respected design talents, and grants a rare opportunity to study the process behind Castiglioni's art. On show are his collection of everyday objects – his 'tools of design instruction', some of which inspired his most celebrated projects – and many of the huge number of photos, prototypes and models that he produced. To visit, you must book in advance for an hourly tour, which take place at 10am, 11am and 12pm Tuesdays to Fridays, and 6.30pm, 7.30pm and 8.30pm on Thursday evenings.
Piazza Castello 27, T 02 805 3606, www.achillecastiglioni.it

Spazio Rossana Orlandi

This two-storey showroom in a former tie factory with a vine-filled garden courtyard displays contemporary and vintage design and also hosts one of the most important and reliably amusing presentations during Salone del Mobile. Rossana Orlandi has helped launch the careers of such globally recognised names as Germans Ermičs, Nika Zupanc and Piet Hein Eek, and continues to exhibit consistently original work. Amid the rows of old tie drawers you might find Maarten Baas' lumpy 'Clay' chairs, colour-diffracting lights by Dennis Parren, Gaetano Pesce's moulded foam foot, or Toronto firm UUfie's flamboyant Corian 'Peacock' chair (above). The neighbouring Bistro Aimo e Nadia (T 02 4802 6205) is a collaboration with the two-Michelin-starred restaurant. *Via Matteo Bandello 14-16, T 02 467 4471, www.rossanaorlandi.com*

Lia Rumma

Near Cimitero Monumentale, essentially an open-air museum containing 150 years of sculpture, Via Stilicone has morphed into a mini arts district as workshops are turned into studios. The forerunner was Fonderia Battaglia (T 02 341 071), a foundry that has cast bronze statues for artists of the calibre of Arnaldo Pomodoro for over a century. Down the street, Lia Rumma hosts thought-provoking works by globally renowned figures such as Anselm Kiefer and Marina Abramović, as well as heavyweight Italians, from Vanessa Beecroft to Marzia Migliora ('Forza Lavoro', above), Giuliano Dal Molin and the estate of Ugo Mulas. Converted by architects CLS, the stark three-storey box is softened by a first-floor terrace and a roof event space. Open Tuesdays to Saturdays. *Via Stilicone 19, T 02 2900 0101, www.liarumma.it*

ARCHITOUR

A GUIDE TO MILAN'S ICONIC BUILDINGS

It should be said that Milan has never been the first port of call for architecture fans. Apart from the Duomo (see p014), which took 427 years to complete and runs the gamut of styles from Gothic to Renaissance, and its idiosyncratic neighbour, Torre Velasca (see p011), it has otherwise been characterised by blocks of anonymous towers that replaced the bombsites in the postwar boom years.

Yet today a dynamism is pervading the smog, which is itself being redressed with a new environmental awareness and initiatives that embrace sustainability, such as the seven disused rail facilities being turned into parks in the next decade to form a green ring around the city. The government has also been able to finally jump enough political and funding hurdles to cajole some long-stalled projects to completion, notably the renovation of the 1764 Palazzo Citterio (Via Brera 12), on-off since the 1970s, that will incorporate James Stirling's concrete bunker in its conversion into a gallery (see p056).

Individual gems from all eras dot the metropolis, of course. Seek out Palazzo dell'Arengario (see p077), a benchmark of rationalist architecture; Tadao Ando's hauntingly ethereal Teatro Armani (Via Bergognone 59), a factory conversion from 2000; the noughties brutalism of Università Bocconi (see p078); and curiosities like the concrete igloos of Villaggio dei Giornalisti (Via Lepanto). Milan's architectural hero, though, will always be Gio Ponti (opposite). *For full addresses, see Resources.*

Chiesa di San Francesco al Fopponino
Gio Ponti worked in Milan all his life. The Pirelli Tower (see p013) is his best-known legacy, but other notable contributions to the city include his twin offices for the Montecatini company at Via Moscova 3/ Largo Donegani 2, built in 1936 and 1951, and two arresting churches. The Chiesa di San Francesco d'Assisi al Fopponino, a collaboration with Antonio Fornaroli and Alberto Rosselli, was completed in 1964.

The facade is clad in diamond-shaped tiles and set back from the street, with the east and west wings recessed further, providing a screen for the courtyards behind. The configuration of the tiles and hexagonal windows are typical Ponti motifs; those to either side of the nave are open, framing the sky. Ponti's Chiesa dell'Ospedale San Carlo Borromeo, from 1966, is on Via Pio II. *Via Giovio 41, www.fopponino.it*

Fondazione Giangiacomo Feltrinelli

Once-rundown Porta Volta is undergoing a renewal marked most prominently by the dramatic Fondazione Feltrinelli, unveiled in 2016. Designed by Herzog & de Meuron, its steeply pitched roof cuts a jagged profile yet seems to meld into the surroundings and the sky, thanks to the reflective glass, while the elongated footprint pays homage to traditional Lombardy *cascine* (communal farmhouses). The publishing company that is headquartered here was founded in 1954 by Giangiacomo Feltrinelli, a leftist agitator who was killed in mysterious circumstances in 1972. It hosts a café and bookstore and, at the gabled top level, a reading room that offers fine views. In the basement, a huge archive of historical documents, including postwar political posters, is fascinating. *Viale Pasubio 5, T 02 495 8341, www.fondazionefeltrinelli.it*

Fiera Milano

Next to the Expo site, a 25-minute metro ride from the city centre, Massimiliano and Doriana Fuksas' 2005 trade-fair complex was part of a massive regeneration project. Built on the grounds of an old oil refinery in just 24 months at a cost of €750m, the exhibition area alone covers 345,000 sq m. The central element is a ribbon-like glass-and-steel canopy that stretches for 1.3km, enveloping the buildings along its path. It ends in a crater-like vortex at either side. Several innovative solutions were devised to help keep the development as green as possible. Perhaps the most interesting is the photocatalytic paint that was used to treat the pavilions: the 100,000 sq m of coated surfaces is said to neutralise the air pollution produced by 15,000 cars. *Strada Statale del Sempione 28, T 02 49 971, www.fieramilano.it*

Museo del Novecento

The city's post-1900 art collection was in storage for more than a decade until 2010 when it was given a home in the converted Palazzo dell'Arengario, a fascist-era relic adorned with lovely bas reliefs by Arturo Martini that was not completed until 1956. Architects Italo Rota and Fabio Fornasari conceived a discreet, light-filled structure incorporating a spiralling indoor ramp that connects the ground level to a terrace

overlooking Piazza del Duomo, and swish restaurant/bar Giacomo Arengario (T 02 7209 3814). A covered walkway leads to further galleries in the adjacent Palazzo Reale. The permanent collection is superb, with particularly strong sections dedicated to the futurists, spatialism (a whole floor is devoted to Lucio Fontana) and Arte Povera. *Piazza del Duomo, T 02 8844 4061, www.museodelnovecento.org*

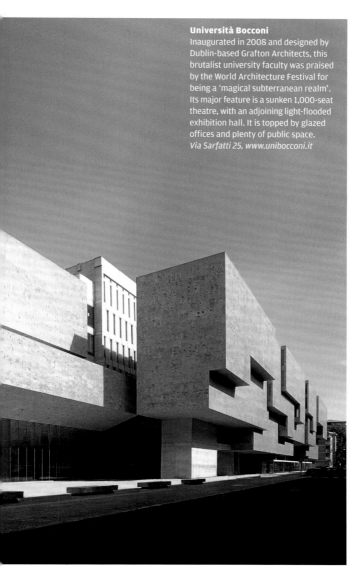

Università Bocconi
Inaugurated in 2008 and designed by
Dublin-based Grafton Architects, this
brutalist university faculty was praised
by the World Architecture Festival for
being a 'magical subterranean realm'.
Its major feature is a sunken 1,000-seat
theatre, with an adjoining light-flooded
exhibition hall. It is topped by glazed
offices and plenty of public space.
Via Sarfatti 25, www.unibocconi.it

SHOPS

THE BEST RETAIL THERAPY AND WHAT TO BUY

One of Milan's top attractions is its shopping, notably around the Quadrilatero of Via Manzoni, Via Montenapoleone, Via della Spiga and Via Sant'Andrea. Luxury brands are here in force, from Missoni (see p094) to Giorgio Armani (Via Montenapoleone 2, T 02 7600 3234), plus local favourites Aspesi (Via Montenapoleone 13, T 02 7602 2478) for quality tailoring, and women's boutiques No 30 (Via della Spiga 30, T 02 7631 7377) and Banner (Via Sant'Andrea 8a, T 02 7600 4609), devised by Gae Aulenti. Close by, the vaulted glass-and-iron arcades of the 1877 Galleria Vittorio Emanuele II have been restored, the bill footed by Prada and Versace. Department store Excelsior (Galleria del Corso 4, T 02 7630 7301), designed by Vincenzo De Cotiis and Jean Nouvel, is its modern equivalent. In Brera, seek out the multibrand Antonia (see p088), and Massimo Piombo (Piazza San Marco 4, T 02 7862 5718) for menswear.

Around Via Durini, you will find the design heavyweights such as B&B Italia (No 14, T 02 764 441) and Flos (Corso Monforte 15, T 02 3701 1080), though there are excellent interiors showrooms spread throughout the city – make a beeline for Fragile (see p082) and Spotti (Viale Piave 27, T 02 781 953). In Zona Tortona, check out Antonio Marras' concept store, Nonostante Marras (Via Cola di Rienzo 8, T 02 8907 5002), and browse the antiques market held on the last Sunday of the month along the Naviglio Grande canal. *For full addresses, see Resources.*

Nilufar Depot

Nina Yashar launched the intimate Nilufar Gallery (T 02 780 193) in Via della Spiga in 1979, initially as a showcase for seminal 20th-century design and oriental carpets, later championing emerging talent. For the past three decades, she has been compiling stock in a vast hangar in the north, which she opened in 2015 as Nilufar Depot, after an overhaul inspired by Teatro alla Scala by local architect Massimiliano Locatelli.

A triple-height cement-floored atrium is surrounded by mises en scène framed by black metal supports, allowing for a survey of 3,000 pieces. Work by contemporary talents that Yashar has long supported, such as Martino Gamper, Lindsey Adelman, Roberto Baciocchi and Cristina Celestino, is mixed among midcentury masterpieces. *Viale Lancetti 34, T 02 3659 0800, www.nilufar.com*

Fragile

A colourful repudiation of the minimal design-gallery scene, Fragile, with its mint-green walls and puzzle-pattern tiled floor, is a supercharged three-level space dreamt up by Atelier Mendini. It sells work by the 20th-century's rowdier figures, such as Gino Sarfatti, Gio Ponti and Franco Albini, and vintage jewellery. *Via San Damiano 2, T 02 3656 1161, www.fragilemilano.com*

Marni

The flagship of this homegrown label, in an Italianate building in a pretty ochre-hued courtyard, was unveiled in 2015 with an interior devised by founder Consuelo Castiglioni and regular collaborator Luz Maria Jaramillo. The fit-out is as good as the clothes and embodies the same vision: arty, architectural and polychromatic, with a clever mashing of materials, textures, structure and shape. On our visit, arcing chrome rails were showcasing boxy, short-sleeve shirts, slightly egg-shaped leather dustcoats and oversized cotton dresses in striped poplin. A cast-concrete parapet swoops down to a subterranean floor, and carpets are adorned with geometric patterns in peach, navy, chocolate and sage green – a distinctly Marni palette.
Via Montenapoleone 12, T 02 7631 7327, www.marni.com

Arthur Arbesser

Since 2013, womenswear designer Arthur Arbesser has been creating sophisticated, gently tailored garments, often in punchy, eccentric colours, which draw conceptually on his Austrian heritage, yet feel Milanese due to the use of fine Italian fabrics. A 2018 collection referenced the Vienna Secession artist Koloman Moser — his ceramics and blown-glass vessels were the inspiration for metallic pastel A-line skirts and shiny trench coats. Painterly, abstract prints have adorned softly ballooning dresses but the main recurring motif is geometric, from grids to stripes and arches, as seen in the classic chequerboard print on this pleated silk-viscose shirt (above), €295. Select pieces are available at the playful, chic lifestyle boutique Wait and See (T 02 7208 0195), situated in a former convent. *www.arthurarbesser.com*

Slam Jam

Born in Luca Benini's garage in 1989 and later based in Navigli until 2016, streetwear emporium Slam Jam now occupies a multi-levelled store inside the former Mazzotta Foundation. Designed by Andrea Caputo, the industrial-tinged interior has redwood shelving, plexiglass display units, concrete flooring and perforated metal sheeting. The offering is international, with a focus on harder-to-find, interesting brands, for instance, Bianca Chandôn, Undercover, Aries and Craig Green. Look out for the Italian labels, such as Napapijri and Kappa Kontroll, and Super by Retrosuperfuture eyeware, often collaborations with the likes of Gosha Rubchinskiy. There are also accessories, such as caps by Stone Island, and books, magazines and records.
Via Giovanni Lanza 1, T 02 8909 3965, www.slamjam.com

Antonia
For Antonia Giacinti's boutique of mens-
and womenswear, go-to-guy Vincenzo
De Cotiis stripped back the stone walls
of a 19th-century palazzo to contrast
with his gleaming lights and furnishings.
Look for speciality pieces from Fendi
and Balenciaga, accessories by Valextra
and Borsalino, and young labels Alanui,
Department Five and Marcelo Burlon.
Via Cusani 5, T 02 8699 8340

Sunnei

Loris Messina and Simone Rizzo (see p054) established their menswear brand in 2014. The store/atelier was designed by Studio Modulo, and features a raw-edged circular hole that visually connects the two spaces, Alvar Aalto 'Model 66' chairs and chenille curtains. The pared-back interior leaves the emphasis on the spirited, subversive garments, from tees to knits, trousers and outerwear, which hang beside accessories such as oversized totes and sabot-style sneakers. Sunnei predominantly uses old-school fabrics manufactured in traditional factories in Veneto. And while items like the loose-cut wool gabardine trousers, a streamlined jacket with detachable sleeves and a denim PVC trench are youth-centric, they are always exquisitely tailored. *Via Vincenzo Vela 8, T 02 2951 1728, www.sunnei.it*

Antica Barbieria Colla

Founded in 1904, this institution has been keeping the local gentry preened for over a century. The barbershop moved to its current premises behind La Scala in 1944 after it was bombed in the war, bringing the surviving Scuderi e Figlio leather and laminated plastic chairs. Drop by for a hot-towel shave, manicure or short back and sides, and check out the original grooming products made using natural ingredients, such as almond shampoo, jojoba oil beard conditioning balm, capsicum and menthol lotion, and green tobacco aftershave milk. There are four scents: Colonia Nº 4 (above), €105 for 100ml, has notes of lemon, neroli, rosemary, lavender, jasmine, cedarwood and coumarin. Closed Sundays, Mondays, for lunch, and during the holidays.
Via Gerolamo Morone 3, T 02 874 312,
www.anticabarbieriacolla.it

Studiopepe

Arianna Lelli Mami and Chiara Di Pinto founded their interior design agency in 2006, and now also create furniture and items for the home characterised by a sharp sense of colour, surprising palettes, playful geometry and a retro feel. Pieces often juxtapose materials and textures, evident in their 'Hello Sonia' wall hanging, which is comprised of Himalayan wool, silk and brass. We were taken with the ceramic 'Kora' vase (above), €195, inspired by the poise of ancient Greek statues, expressed through an asymmetrical silhouette and accentuated angles. You can order direct (T 02 3650 5993), or find Studiopepe's muted rugs at CC-Tapis (T 02 8909 3884), alongside patterns by Patricia Urquiola, Martino Gamper and Federico Pepe, all of which are made by hand in Nepal. *www.studiopepedesign.it*

Lorenzi by Larusmiani

Cutler G Lorenzi had been trading on Via Montenapoleone since 1929, until rising rents forced its closure in 2014. Thankfully, neighbouring retailer Guglielmo Miani, president of Larusmiani – a tailoring and lifestyle brand, and similarly a Milanese institution – offered Lorenzi space in the basement. Housed in antique walnut and burlwood cabinets are 20,000 pieces (the collection previously topped 100,000, with 300 different models of hairbrush alone), including blades, grooming tools, cufflink boxes, nutcrackers and even picnic sets, all selected by Giovanni's son Aldo Lorenzi, who has since retired. As for the future, Miani hopes to devise new product lines with a similar level of refinement. *Via Montenapoleone 7, T 02 7600 6957, www.larusmiani.it/it/collections/ lorenzi-by-larusmiani.html*

Missoni

Patricia Urquiola reimagined Missoni's headline store, bang in the epicentre of the Quadrilatero, in collaboration with the label's creative director, Angela Missoni, who took over from her parents, Ottavio and Rosita, in 1997. Adopting the brand's distinctive patterns and textures as the inspiration, they devised a sophisticated, faintly nostalgic scheme of striped panels (very redolent of those signature zigzags), wood panelling and block-colour display units, hanging the high-end knitwear from slender wooden rails. The Missoni legend, born in nearby Varese, celebrated its 65th year in 2018, and is venerated as one of the family-run firms that turned Italian fashion into such a global force. Note that the entrance is actually on Via Sant'Andrea. *Via Montenapoleone 8, T 02 7600 3555, www.missoni.it*

Pavè Gelato

The original Pavè café (T 02 9439 2259) launched in 2012, and gained a reputation for its bread made with stoneground flour, baked goods and, at weekends, *millefoglie espressa*, a cream-filled puff-pastry cake that is made to order in eight minutes. Its three founders branched out in 2016 with Pavè Gelato, which they furnished with repurposed cinema seats, industrial-style lighting and hexagonal floor tiles. The ice cream comes in flavours that borrow from the café – *sbrisolona* (a classic Lombardy recipe), buttered toast with jam, or tarte tatin, for example – alongside a number of seasonal treats, among them pistachio, cardamom, tonka bean and hazelnut. The Sicilian citrus granita has become our go-to refreshment on steamy summer days.
*Via Cesare Battisti 21, T 02 876 4530,
www.pavemilano.com/en/ice-cream*

ESCAPES

WHERE TO GO IF YOU WANT TO LEAVE TOWN

The Milanese take full advantage of the city's proximity to the Alps and the coast, and many spend almost every weekend out of town. The lakes offer the quickest escape. Como (see p098) is a 50-minute journey; Lugano, over the Swiss border, is just over an hour; and it is two hours to Garda. All are accessible by rail. Also in the region is Villa Panza (opposite), which, together with Castello di Rivoli (see p102), just outside Turin to the west, shows some of country's best contemporary art. And within striking distance, to the south, is Modena, for chef Massimo Bottura's divine Osteria Francescana (Via Stella 22, T 05 922 3912). It is halfway to Florence, which you can reach in 90 minutes on the high-speed Frecciarossa train.

For a dip in the Med, the Portofino promontory is enchanting, a forested marine park that cosies up to the famous harbour. Nearby is the bay of Paraggi and one of the area's few public beaches, Bagni Fiore (Via Paraggi a Mare 1, Santa Margherita Ligure, T 01 8528 4831), and Camogli, where Fondazione Pier Luigi e Natalina Remotti (Via Castagneto 52, T 01 8577 2137) is a fascinating art space in a deconsecrated church. From Milan, it takes three hours by train. Alternatively, head to a mountain spa like Therme Vals (see p101) or, in South Tyrol, Vigilius Resort (Vigiljoch, Lana, T 04 7355 6600) and Terme Merano (Piazza Terme 9, Merano, T 04 7325 2000). To visit either, catch a train to Bolzano, then it's a 35km taxi ride. *For full addresses, see Resources.*

Villa Panza, Varese

This 18th-century baroque villa an hour north of the city houses Giuseppe Panza di Biumo's extraordinary collection of US art amassed since the 1950s – more than 150 pieces inspired by colour and light. Panza donated a portion of his hoard to global institutions including the Guggenheim in New York but kept the majority here at the family home, opened in 2000 and run by the non-profit FAI. The splendid grounds, dotted with land art, are worth the trip alone. Inside, among the highlights are seven works by Italian minimalist Ettore Spalletti, 11 site-specific installations by Dan Flavin in the Rustici wing (corridor, above), a Robert Irwin piece in the old stables, and James Turrell's immersive, hue-shifting *Ganzfeld – Sight Unseen*. *Piazza Litta 1, T 0332 283 960, www.villapanza.it*

Hotel Il Sereno, Lake Como

On a promontory above sapphire waters ringed by Alpine peaks, Il Sereno, designed by Patricia Urquiola (right down to the staff uniforms), has an enviable perch and style. The 2016 building is a reinterpretation of Giuseppe Terragni's 1936 rationalist Casa del Fascio nearby, using local materials including Pietra di Fossena flooring and Ceppo Lombardo for the facade, and living walls by Patrick Blanc. Inside, a staircase of walnutwood and bronze appears as if it were floating, and lighting by Flos includes fixtures suspended in leather harnesses. Michelin-starred restaurant Berton al Lago is nestled within the ancient stone arches below and spills out onto a lovely terrace, and there's also a spa, manicured gardens, infinity pool, beach and private flotilla. *Via Torrazza 10, Torno, T 031 547 7800, www.serenohotels.com/property/il-sereno*

D'O, Cornaredo

One of Italy's most respected chefs, Davide Oldani, launched D'O in his home town in 2003. It's set in a sleepy piazza and has a Scandi-inflected design by Piero Lissoni, incorporating a perforated metal facade, whitewashed walls and glass balustrades; Oldani stipulated that the oak chairs, made by Como-based Riva 1920, should be 5cm higher than standard to improve digestion. The exemplary fare comprises inventive seasonal creations made using humble ingredients such as a signature rice dish with bread, black pepper and Marsala; broccoli gnocchi with sesame seeds and raisins; and veal with San Pietro cheese and beeswax. A 30-minute taxi ride from Milan towards Malpensa, it makes a fine farewell stop. Closed Sunday and Monday. *Piazza della Chiesa 14, T 02 936 2209, www.cucinapop.do*

Therme Vals, Vals, Switzerland

Milan's proximity to Switzerland means that Therme Vals makes for a pleasant three-and-a-half-hour car ride. Here, Peter Zumthor has used 60,000 slabs of Valser quartzite to create a cathedral to bathing, with indoor and outdoor thermal pools. The use of light and shade, and open and enclosed spaces, enhances the feeling of tranquillity as you take in the health benefits of the spring. Book in advance for the wellness centre, which offers a range of treatments, from masks and exfoliation to wraps and massage. Stay at the interconnected 7132 Hotel (spa entry included), choosing one of the new Kengo Kuma-designed oak cocoons, or at the excellent family guesthouse Hotel Alpina (T +41 819 207 040), where you should reserve a modernised room.
T +41 587 132 000, www.7132therme.com

Castello di Rivoli, Rivoli
The residence of the Savoy royal family from 1247 to 1883, this hilltop castle and palace has a tumultuous history. Mostly dating from the early 18th century, it was repeatedly plundered, occupied by the army, then bombed in WWII. Collapses in 1978 spurred the regional government into action and, with the help of collector Giuseppe Panza (see p097), it was restored by architect Andrea Bruno, and opened as a museum in 1984. Now, original frescoes, paintings, tapestries, stucco and carvings coexist harmoniously with glass-and-steel viewing platforms and brand-new galleries. It is an extraordinary backdrop for large-scale 20th- and 21st-century works from artists including Michelangelo Pistoletto (*Venus of the Rags*, right) and Maurizio Cattelan. An express bus runs from Porta Susa in Turin on weekends and holidays. *Piazza Mafalda di Savoia, T 011 956 5222, www.castellodirivoli.org*

NOTES
SKETCHES AND MEMOS

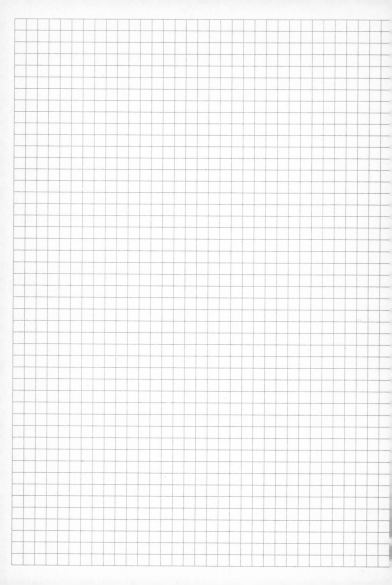

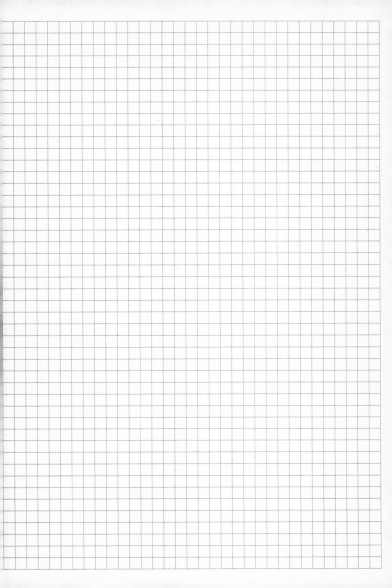

RESOURCES
CITY GUIDE DIRECTORY

HOTELS
ADDRESSES AND ROOM RATES

Hotel Alpina 101
Room rates:
double, €135
Dorfplatz
Vals
Switzerland
T +41 819 207 040
www.hotel-alpina-vals.ch

Armani Hotel 016
Room rates:
double, €660
Via Manzoni 31
T 02 8883 8888
www.armanihotelmilano.com

Bulgari Hotel 017
Room rates:
double, €845;
Premium Suite 416, €3,200;
Bulgari Suite, €5,175
Via Privata Fratelli Gabba 7b
T 02 805 8051
www.bulgarihotels.com

Four Seasons 016
Room rates:
double, €665
Via Gesù 6-8
T 02 77 088
www.fourseasons.com/milan

Magna Pars Suites 016
Room rates:
double, €260
Via Forcella 6
T 02 833 8371
www.magnapars-suitesmilano.it

Palazzo Parigi 016
Room rates:
double, €550
Corso di Porta Nuova 1
T 02 625 625
www.palazzoparigi.com

Palazzo Segreti 022
Room rates:
double, €230;
Junior Design Suite 8, €280
Via San Tomaso 8
T 02 4952 9250
www.palazzosegreti.com

7132 Hotel 101
Room rates:
Kengo Kuma-designed room, €330;
double, €500
Vals
Switzerland
T +41 587 132 000
www.7132.com

Senato Hotel 018
Room rates:
double, €210;
Junior Suite, €290
Via Senato 22
T 02 781 236
www.senatohotelmilano.it

Hotel Il Sereno 098
Room rates:
double, €750
Via Torrazza 10
Torno
Lake Como
T 031 547 7800
www.serenohotels.com/property/
il-sereno

Straf 016
  Room rates:
  double, €220
  Via San Raffaele 3
  T 02 805 081
  www.straf.it
Hotel Viu 020
  Room rates:
  double, €260;
  Viu Suite 701, €3,000
  Via Fioravanti 6
  T 02 8001 0910
  www.hotelviumilan.com
The Yard 023
  Room rates:
  double, €240;
  Maison Wicket, €330
  Piazza XXIV Maggio 8
  T 02 8941 5901
  www.theyardmilano.com

WALLPAPER* CITY GUIDES

Executive Editor
Jeremy Case

Author
Laura Rysman

Photography Editor
Rebecca Moldenhauer

Art Editor
Jade R Arroyo

Editorial Assistant
Charlie Monaghan

Photo Assistant
Daniëlle Siobhán Mol

Sub-editors
Sophie Dening
Emma Barton

Contributors
Emily Paul
Federica Sala
Ed Upright

Interns
Izzie Claridge
Aïsha Diomandé
Lydia Dunton
Laura Ferguson

Milan Imprint
First published 2006
Eighth edition 2018

ISBN 978 0 7148 7652 8

More City Guides
www.phaidon.com/travel

Follow us
@wallpaperguides

Contact
wcg@phaidon.com

Original Design
Loran Stosskopf

Map Illustrator
Russell Bell

Production Controller
Gif Jittiwutikarn

**Assistant Production
Controller**
Sarah Scott

Wallpaper* Magazine
161 Marsh Wall
London E14 9AP
contact@wallpaper.com

Wallpaper*® is a
registered trademark
of TI Media

Phaidon Press Limited
Regent's Wharf
All Saints Street
London N1 9PA

Phaidon Press Inc
65 Bleecker Street
New York, NY 10012

All prices and venue
information are correct
at time of going to press,
but are subject to change.

A CIP Catalogue record for
this book is available from
the British Library.

Phaidon® is a registered
trademark of Phaidon
Press Limited

PHOTOGRAPHERS

MILAN
A COLOUR-CODED GUIDE TO THE CITY'S HOT 'HOODS

MAGENTA
Highlights of this 19th-century district are its stately buildings and the panini at De Santis

SEMPIONE
Within the green expanse of Parco Sempione, head for the 1933 Triennale design museum

PORTA ROMANA
This low-key residential area has some quality local eateries, and the Bagni Misteriosi pool

CENTRO
At the city's very core, Piazza del Duomo is enclosed by iconic architecture from all eras

PORTA VENEZIA
Milan is at its most multicultural here, but Villa Necchi Campiglio is as Italian as it gets

BRERA/MONTENAPOLEONE
A strong gallery and foodie scene is emerging around this nirvana of luxury and fashion

NAVIGLI/ZONA TORTONA
Creatives have injected a buzz into the drinking and dining spots on the canals and beyond

PORTA NUOVA/ISOLA
Many of the statement high-rises cluster in Porta Nuova while Isola is far more laidback

For a full description of each neighbourhood, see the Introduction.
Featured venues are colour-coded, according to the district in which they are located.